Let's Learn About

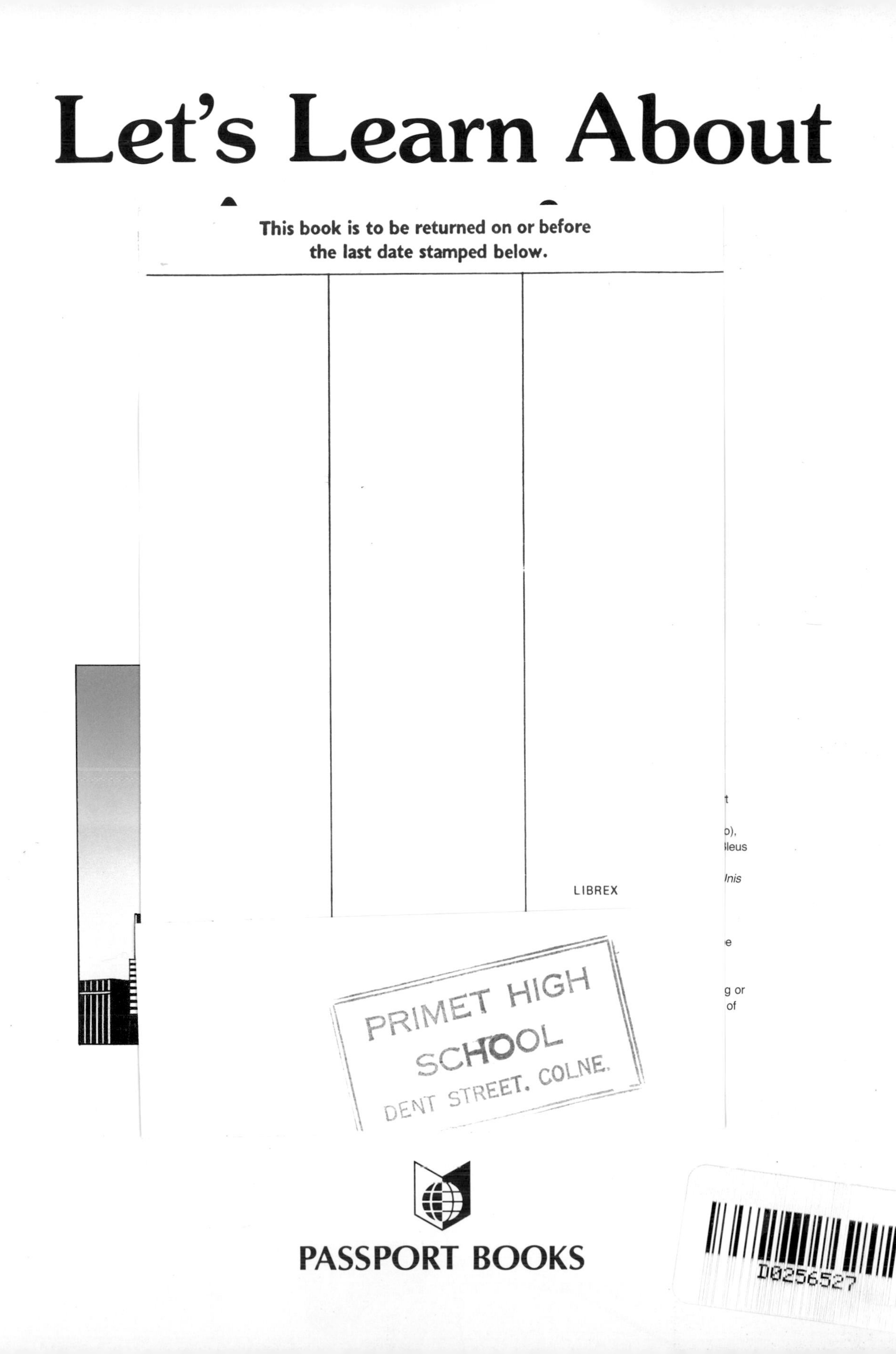

PASSPORT BOOKS

USA at a glance

The United States spans an entire continent with more than 230 million people of every race and color.

See how the time changes as you cross the country from east to west! Read the clocks to answer our questions. If it is noon in New York, what time is it in London and in San Francisco?

Solution: It is 5 P.M. in London and 9 A.M. in San Francisco.

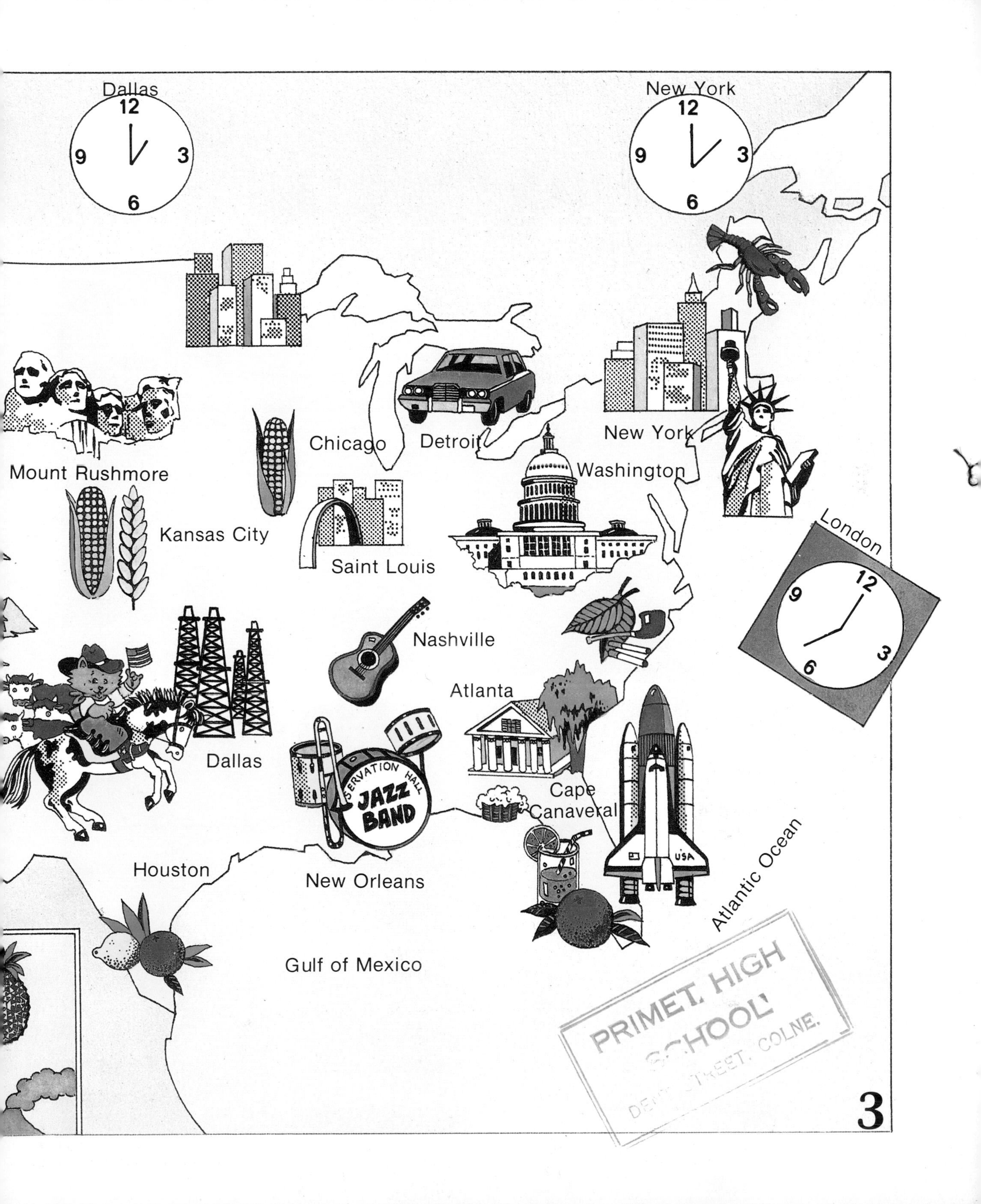
Dallas
New York
Mount Rushmore
Chicago
Detroit
New York
Washington
Kansas City
Saint Louis
London
Nashville
Atlanta
Dallas
SERVATION HALL
JAZZ BAND
Cape Canaveral
USA
Atlantic Ocean
Houston
New Orleans
Gulf of Mexico

American landscapes

The American landscape is incredibly varied, as it stretches from the Arctic Circle to the tropical islands of Hawaii. Look at all these animals and decide which landscape is their natural home.

Solution: Prairies = prairie dog, buffalo, pronghorn antelope. Mountains = grouse, bighorn, grizzly bear. Desert = rattlesnake, coyote. Forest = chipmunk, squirrel, raccoon, skunk. Arctic Circle = polar bear. Swamp = alligator.

Solution: (Big) Apple

Solution: the sheriff's badge, film coming out of the movie camera, the wrench, the funnel.

America, America
In 1620, the Pilgrims left England on the "Mayflower" to found the colony of Massachusetts.
The settlers in the South needed workers for their cotton fields and began to bring in slaves from Africa.
On July 4, 1776, the 13 colonies of the New World declared their independence and became the United States of America.
The War of Independence, between the American revolutionaries and the British Red Coats, lasted 5 years.
Here are several important events in U.S. history. Did you notice that something appears in each picture? Look carefully!
8

The early settlers set off to conquer the Wild West.
The native American Indians were pushed farther and farther back by the settlers and were finally forced to live on reservations.
In 1861, the Civil War broke out: the Northern states against the Southern states. After the victory of the North, President Lincoln abolished slavery.
In 1944, the American army landed in France to help liberate Europe and end World War II.
In 1969, Neil Armstrong became the first man to set foot on the moon!
Solution: Stars.

Stars and stripes

The Fourth of July is the most important holiday in the United States. It celebrates the signing of the Declaration of Independence, in 1776.

On the American flag, the 13 stripes stand for the original founding states, while the stars indicate the number of states today. Compare the two flags above. How many states were there in 1776 and how many are there today?

Trick or treat?

Once a year, on October 31, children dress up in costumes to go "trick or treating." They knock on people's doors and offer protection from nasty tricks in exchange for a treat. It is Halloween night, and grinning pumpkins light up yards and windows. To make your own jack-o'-lantern simply cut off the top of a pumpkin and empty it out with a spoon. Then cut out the eyes, nose and mouth and put a candle inside. After dark, you can let your pumpkin face glow mysteriously in your bedroom window.

All-American feast

When the first settlers arrived, the Indians introduced them to plants and animals that did not exist in Europe. Here are a few of them: what are they called and in which dish or product are they used?

Solution: chili = kidney beans; cornflakes and corn on the cob = corn; peanut butter = peanuts; Thanksgiving dinner = turkey; cigarettes = tobacco; pumpkin pie = pumpkin.

Something went wrong here! All the names of these American treats have been jumbled up. You probably know most of them, so put the labels where they belong. Now give all the treats a star rating to show how much you like them:

* = good ** = very good *** = extra special

Solution: A = apple pie; B = brownies; C = cola; D = doughnut; E = eggs and sausages; F = fudge; G = gum; H = hamburger; I = ice cream; J = Halloween candy; K = ketchup; L = lobster; M = marshmallows; N = nuts; O = oatmeal; P = caramel corn; Q = quiche; R = root beer; S = sweet corn; T = taco; U = upside-down cake; V = vanilla sundae; W = waffle; X = foot-long hot dog; Y = yams; Z = zucchini.

At the arcade

All across the country kids love to play video games, pinball machines, and other electronic games found at amusement parks and arcades.

Each fruit here stands for a letter. Try to break the code and discover the message hidden on each of these slot machines.

Solution: good luck; hello guys; how much; let's go

3.2.1
Lift off!
1
2
4
3
2
1
4
3
2
1

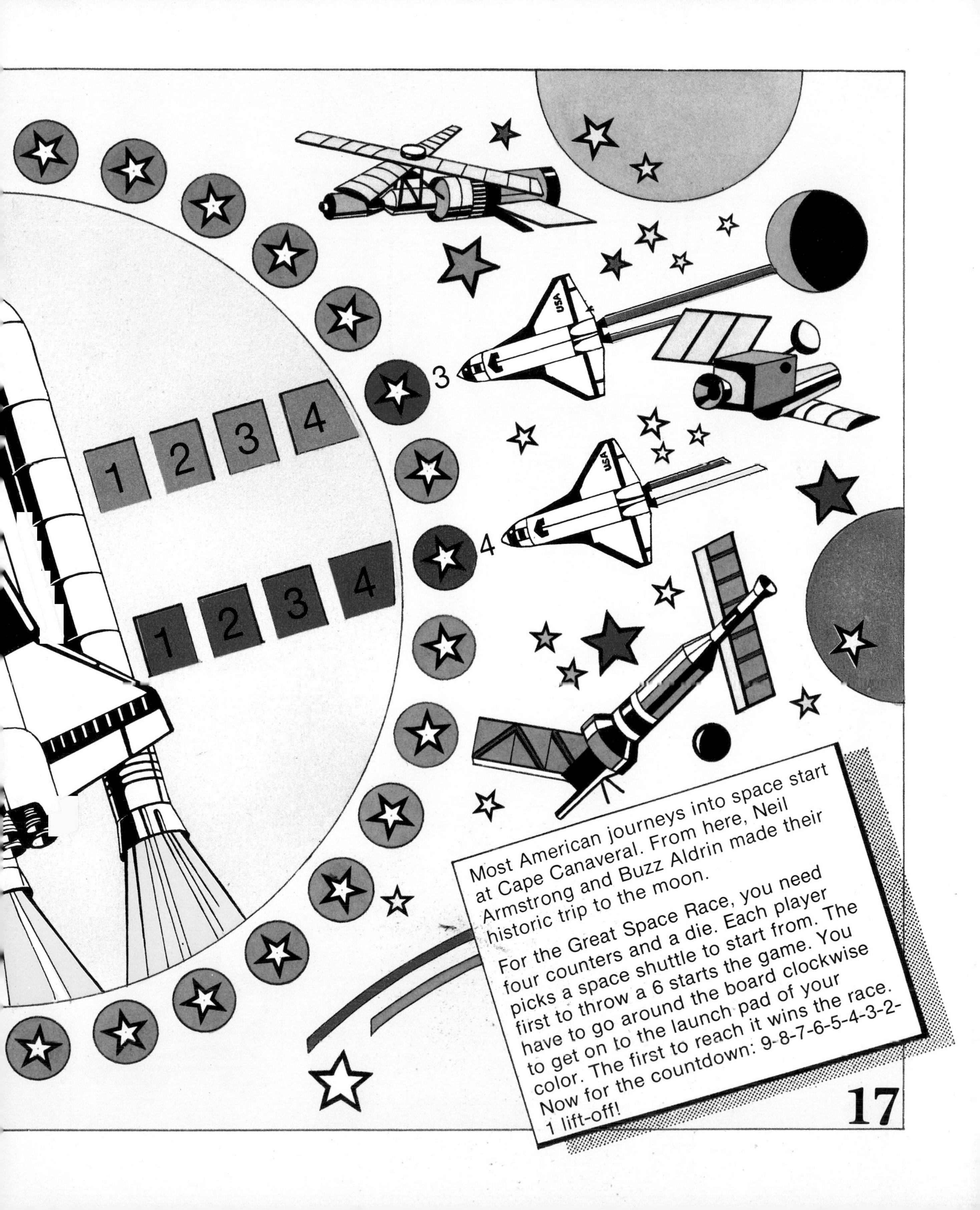

Most American journeys into space start at Cape Canaveral. From here, Neil Armstrong and Buzz Aldrin made their historic trip to the moon.

For the Great Space Race, you need four counters and a die. Each player picks a space shuttle to start from. The first to throw a 6 starts the game. You have to go around the board clockwise to get on to the launch pad of your color. The first to reach it wins the race. Now for the countdown: 9-8-7-6-5-4-3-2-1 lift-off!

Rah! rah! rah!

All these sports were invented in the United States. Do you know what their names are? Figure out what sports equipment each of the people in the picture needs.

Solution: roller skating, kayak racing, baseball, basketball, football, surfing

Baseball is America's national sport. The playing area is made up of an outfield and infield. The infield is diamond shaped, with a pitcher's mound in the middle and 4 bases (first, second, third and home) at each point of the diamond. Each team has 9 players, who all take turns at bat. The pitcher throws the ball to the batter, who has to hit it as far as possible and try to run around the bases before the other team gets the ball and throws him out.

Now it's your turn to spot 5 geometric shapes on this page as quickly as possible.

Getting away!

During their history, Americans have used all these vehicles, first, to conquer the land and, later on, space.

Try putting them in order: from the oldest to the newest. The letters and numbers will tell you how to go west.

Solution: On Route 66

America is the land of big cars, giant superhighways and races for anything on wheels: trucks, tractors and dragsters—crazy custom-built cars.

Who is going to win this race?

Solution: Number 3

Cowboys and Indians

The Indians were America's original inhabitants. The arrival of European settlers had terrible effects on the Indian tribes. Indians died by the thousands because of diseases brought by Europeans and were also massacred. Today, those that remain live on reservations, mostly in Oklahoma, Arizona and New Mexico. Which of these headdresses are the same?

Solution: B and D

Cowboys watch over huge herds of cattle on the prairies of the West.

The cowboys here galloped off in a hurry and left a few things behind. Can you complete their outfits?

Solution: (from left to right) pistol, chaps, spur, glove

Rubbing noses with the Eskimos

lemming

wolf

walrus

penguin

moose

A1417

Alaska is in the northwest part of the continent. Because the Arctic Circle cuts across the state, it has a polar climate: for many months it is covered by a thick blanket of ice and snow. Alaska is the biggest of the states, but it has the smallest population. For centuries, it has been the home of Eskimos, Aleutians and Indians, who live mostly from hunting, fishing and tourism. But the discovery of oil has brought many changes to the state. These often conflict with traditional ways. All these animals except one live in Alaska. Which one is it?

Solution: Penguins live at the South Pole.

In the winter, Eskimos bundle up in thick, fur-lined clothes. For transportation they use sleds or snowmobiles. When they go on a hunt, they camp out in igloos made from snow blocks, but otherwise they live in modern houses.

These Eskimo children have put on their traditional costumes for a special occasion. Find the 5 differences between their outfits.

Rock around the clock!

America is the home of most modern music styles: country music, blues, jazz, rock 'n' roll...

The guitar is the star instrument in all of these, but each type of music has its own special guitar. Find the right guitar for each player.

Solution: A2, B3, C1

American heroes

Meet some famous characters from American books and movies. You'll certainly recognize the titles of their stories once you've untangled them.

Solution: Gone with the Wind; The Last of the Mohicans; Uncle Tom's Cabin; Tom Sawyer; Huckleberry Finn; Davy Crockett; Rin Tin Tin

Dreams come true in Hollywood—at least on the screen. You've seen the movies; now let's gaze at the stars. Can you put the right name on each of these silhouettes?

Solution: The Pink Panther; Donald Duck; Fred Astaire; Droopy; Popeye; Marilyn Monroe; Woody Woodpecker; Tweety Pie; Charlie Chaplin

Made in the USA

Kids all over the world have things in common with American kids: they listen to the same music, they see the same movies and they love hamburgers, popcorn and Coke!

Now look at all these pictures of people and things from everyday life in America—and find the foreign intruders.

Solution: There is a Canadian Mountie,
a Spanish stamp and an English coin.

Reach for the sky!

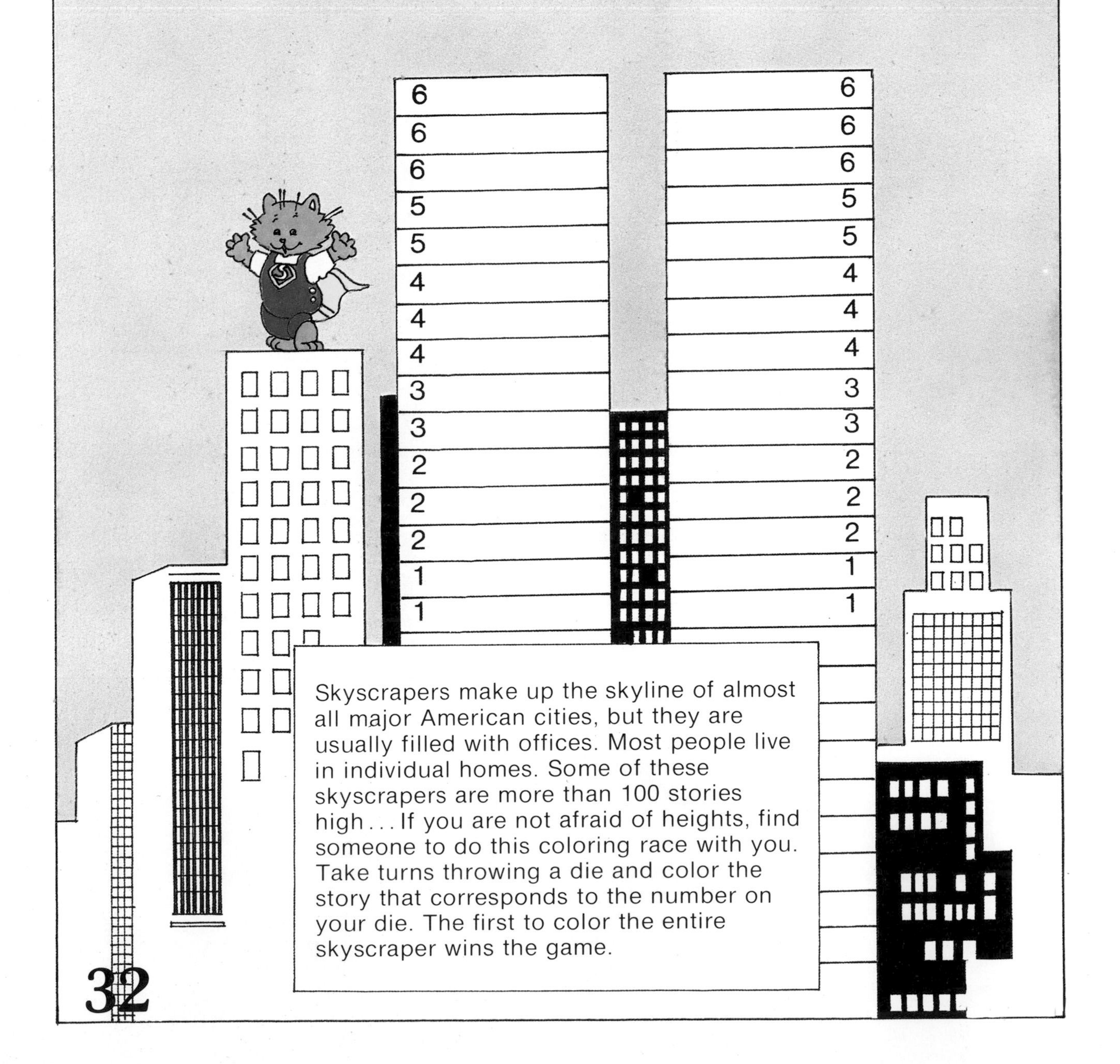

Skyscrapers make up the skyline of almost all major American cities, but they are usually filled with offices. Most people live in individual homes. Some of these skyscrapers are more than 100 stories high . . . If you are not afraid of heights, find someone to do this coloring race with you. Take turns throwing a die and color the story that corresponds to the number on your die. The first to color the entire skyscraper wins the game.